CIVIC PARTICIPATION
Working for Civil Rights

MEXICAN AMERICAN CIVIL RIGHTS MOVEMENT

Christine Honders

PowerKiDS press.

New York

Published in 2017 by The Rosen Publishing Group, Inc.
29 East 21st Street, New York, NY 10010

First Edition

Editor: Caitie McAneney
Book Design: Mickey Harmon

Photo Credits: Cover (image) David Fenton/Contributor/Archive Photos/Getty Images; cover, pp. 1, 3–32 (background) Milena_Bo/Shutterstock.com; p. 5 Bill Peters/Contributor/Denver Post/Getty Images; pp. 7, 9 (main) Everett Historical/Shutterstock.com; p. 9 (inset) https://upload.wikimedia.org/wikipedia/commons/9/91/Juan_Nepomuceno_Cortina.jpg; p. 11 UniversalImagesGroup/Contributor/Universal Images Group/Getty Images; p. 13 https://en.wikipedia.org/wiki/Mendez_v._Westminster#/media/File:SchoolLunch.jpg; p. 15 https://commons.wikimedia.org/wiki/File:Edward_R_Roybal.jpg; pp. 17, 21 Bettmann/Contributor/Bettmann/Getty Images; p. 19 Bill Johnson/Denver Post/Getty Images; p. 23 (Dolores Huerta) Cathy Murphy/Contributor/Hulton Archive/Getty Images; p. 23 (Cesar Chavez) Bob Olsen/Contributor/Toronto Star/Getty Images; p. 25 Annie Wells/Contributor/Los Angeles Times/Getty Images; p. 27 Rod Rolle/Contributor/Hulton Archive/Getty Images; p. 29 ESB Professional/Shutterstock.com.

Library of Congress Cataloging-in-Publication Data

Names: Honders, Christine, author.
Title: Mexican American Civil Rights Movement / Christine Honders.
Description: New York : PowerKids Press, 2017. | Series: Civic participation: working for civil rights | Includes index.
Identifiers: LCCN 2016037023| ISBN 9781499426847 (pbk. book) | ISBN 9781499428520 (library bound book) | ISBN 9781499426830 (6 pack)
Subjects: LCSH: Mexican Americans–Civil rights–History–Juvenile literature. | Civil rights movements–United States–History–Juvenile literature. | United States–Race relations–Juvenile literature.
Classification: LCC E184.M5 H65 2017 | DDC 323.1168/72073–dc23
LC record available at https://lccn.loc.gov/2016037023

Manufactured in the United States of America

CPSIA Compliance Information: Batch #BW17PK: For Further Information contact Rosen Publishing, New York, New York at 1-800-237-9932

CONTENTS

MEXICAN AMERICAN FIGHT FOR CIVIL RIGHTS

Even before the end of the U.S.-Mexican War in 1848, Mexican Americans had to fight to secure their civil rights in the United States. Today, thanks to strong leaders and committed **activists**, Mexican Americans have come a long way in their struggle for rights and representation in the U.S. government.

Civil rights are the basic rights guaranteed to U.S. citizens. These include the right to vote, to receive equal treatment in public places, and to have equal **access** to education, housing, and jobs. For many years, Mexican Americans didn't have these rights. In the 1960s and 1970s, the Mexican American civil rights movement worked to overcome **stereotypes** and fight for the same privileges as all U.S. citizens.

The fight that was started decades ago continues today. People of Mexican descent, especially **undocumented** immigrants, face many struggles in the United States.

MEXICANS IN THE UNITED STATES

Many Mexican Americans lived in the present-day U.S. Southwest during the late 1800s. That's because much of that land used to belong to Mexico. Today, the region includes all or part of the states of California, New Mexico, Texas, Arizona, Utah, Nevada, Colorado, and Wyoming.

This area was greatly affected by the U.S.-Mexican War. The war started because of disagreement over Texas's border after it joined the United States in 1845. After the war ended in 1848, the United States acquired more than 500,000 square miles (1,294,994 sq km) from Mexico. The land was called the Mexican Cession, and it greatly expanded the United States.

The Mexican people living in this conquered territory weren't sure what was going to happen to them. Their ancestors claimed the land many years before. Now they had to live side by side with their conquerors.

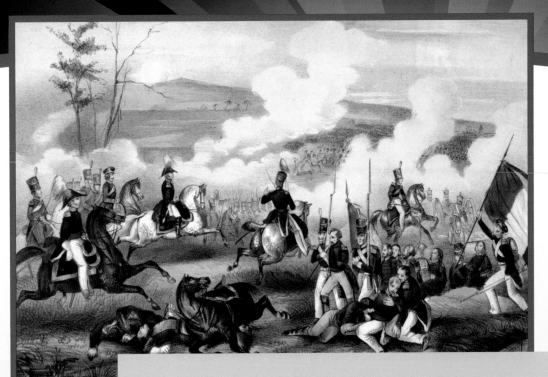

This artwork shows the Battle of Palo Alto, which took place on May 8, 1846, near today's Brownsville, Texas. This was the first major battle of the U.S.-Mexican War.

The Treaty of Guadalupe Hidalgo

The Treaty of Guadalupe Hidalgo was signed in 1848 after the U.S.-Mexican War. It guaranteed constitutional rights for Mexican people living in conquered lands. The treaty stated that people of Mexican descent living in these lands must either leave or join the United States and abandon their Mexican loyalties. It also promised that those who stayed would be given the freedoms and rights of all U.S. citizens under the Constitution. Unfortunately, many people still wouldn't accept them into American society.

RACIAL TENSION ERUPTS

For years after the war there was **racism** against Mexicans who decided to stay within the new borders, even though they were now citizens. Americans were traveling from the East to settle in these new western lands, and they began to outnumber people of Mexican descent. Many people in the United States believed in the idea of Manifest Destiny, which said that it was the fate of the nation to stretch across North America. This belief also made many Americans feel that they had the right to take these lands in any way they could.

Some Americans took the land by reporting to the government that the Mexican Americans were being disloyal. Some used the legal system to cheat the Mexican Americans, many of whom didn't speak English, out of their land. Others resorted to violence against Mexican Americans.

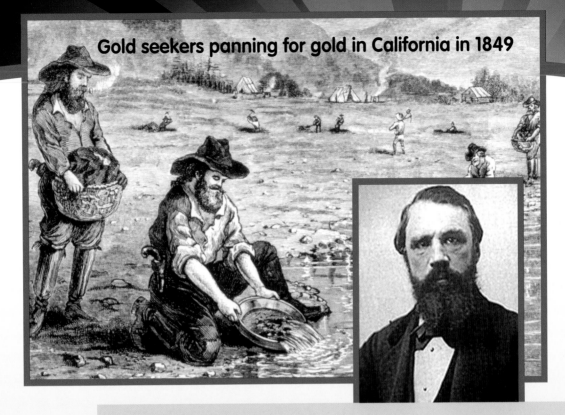

Gold seekers panning for gold in California in 1849

Juan Cortina, pictured here, was a rebel leader in Texas. In the mid-1800s, he vowed to protect Mexican Americans' freedom and rights from the white settlers.

Violence Against Mexican Americans

The gold rush of 1849 brought thousands of white miners to California. Many of these miners removed Mexican Americans from their land by force or by murder. Mexican Americans were often hung for committing crimes, even when there was no proof of guilt. Since law enforcement was either unwilling or unable to protect them, groups of Mexican rebel "bandits" were established in an attempt to scare the newcomers away and take back what was rightfully theirs.

IMMIGRATION AND RACE WARS

In the late 1800s, railroads, farming, and mining were becoming booming industries in the American West. More workers were needed. Mexicans traveled north of the border to find a growing number of jobs that paid higher wages.

The Mexican Revolution brought another wave of immigrants to the United States in 1910. This led to more violence on the U.S.-Mexican border as the United States enforced tougher immigration laws. Newspaper coverage of the violence contributed to greater fear and **discrimination** against those of Mexican descent.

Texas Rangers

Texas was brimming with tension between Mexican Americans and white settlers. Members of the Texas Rangers, a state law enforcement agency, committed some of the most violent attacks against Mexican Americans in the early 1900s. Mexican Americans in Texas were constantly under suspicion and weren't allowed to go out after dark. The rangers committed and allowed many shootings and hangings. By 1919, about 5,000 Mexican Americans in Texas had been killed and thousands more had been driven off their land.

On March 9, 1916, Mexican revolutionary Pancho Villa led his men in an attack in the border town of Columbus, New Mexico. General John J. Pershing led his troops into Mexico to find Villa. However, Villa escaped and became a Mexican hero.

In 1915, a group of Mexican Americans living in Texas created the "Plan of San Diego" to free Southwest states from U.S. control. It called for a bloody revolution. While the revolution never happened, there were dozens of raids in 1915 and 1916 by Mexican Americans and their allies.

RACIAL SEGREGATION

The increase in Mexican and European immigrants coming into the United States also led to racial **segregation** throughout the southwestern states. Many Mexican immigrants were unskilled workers and very poor, and they were targeted by the middle-class Anglo Americans. Local businesses put up signs that said "No Mexicans Allowed" or "Whites Only."

Segregated schools became common in states such as California and Texas, where there were separate buildings called "Mexican schools." The government allowed this, saying that Mexican American children needed a special environment where they could be taught English. However, these children didn't receive any special attention. Instead, they had older books, fewer teachers and lessons, and some of the most rundown school buildings.

Just as policies called "black codes" legalized segregation against African Americans in the South, similar laws and policies discriminated against Mexican Americans in the Southwest.

Students eat lunch at school in Peñasco, New Mexico

THE ROOTS OF THE MOVEMENT

In 1929, several groups combined to form the League of United Latin American Citizens (LULAC). Its purpose was to end discrimination and to promote education for Mexican Americans. Around the same time, Mexican American workers at farms, mines, and factories, tired of the poor treatment on the job, joined the fight to form labor unions. Today, LULAC is the oldest Latino civil rights group in the United States.

The early victories in the movement were mostly in the courts. In 1947, in the court case of *Mendez v. Westminster*, a judge ruled that segregated schools in Orange County, California, were against the 14th Amendment of the U.S. Constitution. This amendment, or addition to the constitution, granted citizenship and equal protection under the law to all Americans.

Edward Roybal

People use the words "Latino" or "Latina" to describe a person of Latin American descent who lives in the United States. The word "Hispanic" refers to a person from a Spanish-speaking background. These words are sometimes used to mean the same thing, but it's important to know their differences and what people prefer to be called.

A Win for Hispanic Voters

In 1947, a group called the Community Service Organization (CSO) was created to encourage Mexican Americans in Southern California to register to vote. With about 15,000 newly registered Hispanic voters, Mexican Americans were finally able to win elections. Edward Roybal became the first Mexican American congressman from California, and Cruz Reynoso was the first Latino to sit on the California State Supreme Court.

THE CHICANO MOVEMENT

The fight for Mexican American civil rights started to make real progress in the early 1960s. The African American civil rights movement had already gotten the country's attention. Now, Mexican American youth—who experienced segregation in schools—were ready to push their movement ahead.

Before the movement the term "Chicano" had often been used as a hurtful word to describe children of Mexican migrants. Younger Mexican American activists decided to use the name as a symbol of determination and pride in their Mexican roots. The Mexican American civil rights movement also became known as the Chicano movement, or El Movimiento. Its focus was on voting and political rights, educational equality, farm workers' rights, and **land grants** that were never honored by the U.S. government.

Mexican Americans hold a rally in Sacramento, California, in 1971. Protesters marched from the city of Calexico all the way to Sacramento to protest discrimination. The journey took about three months to complete. This march is known as La Marcha de la Reconquista.

A Fair Voting Process

The Voting Rights Act of 1965 was supposed to end discrimination by making sure that **minorities** would be treated fairly during the voting process. However, its main focus was on African Americans in the South, who also suffered from a great deal of racism and violence. It took years for members of the Hispanic community to convince the government that they needed protection too. Finally, in 1975, Mexican Americans were included in the Voting Rights Act, and voting ballots became available in Spanish.

RODOLFO "CORKY" GONZALES

    Rodolfo "Corky" Gonzales was an important leader of the Chicano movement. After a career as a boxer, he became interested in politics. He ran for state representative in Colorado and lost, then worked on voter registration during John F. Kennedy's presidential campaign. He was very successful and registered more Mexican Americans in Colorado than had ever been registered before.

    When President Lyndon B. Johnson's War on Poverty legislation, or laws, passed in 1964, Gonzales took a job as director of the Denver's War on Poverty office. In 1966, he established the Crusade for Justice in Denver, which provided jobs, healthcare, and legal services for Mexican Americans. He also marched with the Poor People's Campaign in 1968. He wrote the poem *I Am Joaquin*, which came to represent the spirit of the Chicano movement.

This is a section from the poem *I Am Joaquin*: "I am Joaquín, lost in a world of confusion, caught up in the whirl of a gringo [white] society, confused by the rules . . . and destroyed by modern society."

Lifelong Leader

Gonzales earned the nickname "Corky" when he was a child from an uncle who said that he "was always popping off like a cork." Gonzales once confronted a U.S. attorney general and asked him to do something to stop the discrimination against Mexican Americans in housing, the workplace, and schools. He also helped organize a student walkout in protest of racist remarks that were made by a teacher at West High School in Denver.

LA ALIANZA

Nicknamed "King Tiger," Reies López Tijerina was another force in the Chicano movement. When Tijerina was a young boy in Texas, his grandfather was nearly killed by white racists. This shaped his political views for life. In the late 1950s and early 1960s, Tijerina joined a group of people in New Mexico whose ancestors' lands had been taken in **violation** of the Treaty of Guadalupe Hidalgo after the U.S.-Mexican War. The group called upon Mexican officials to act on their behalf, but they were unsuccessful.

Tijerina continued to research land grants and, in 1963, he started La Alianza Federal de Mercedes (Federal Alliance of Land Grants). In October 1966, members of La Alianza took over a rock formation in New Mexico called the Echo Amphitheater, which they claimed was on land stolen by the United States. They renamed the land the Republic of San Joaquín.

Reies López Tijerina

Tijerina became the Latino leader of the 1968 Poor People's Campaign.

Trespassing

La Alianza tried to arrest two forest rangers for trespassing in the Republic of San Joaquín. They also demanded that the federal government prove who owned the land. After five days, members of La Alianza turned themselves in, and Tijerina and others were arrested for attacking government officials. In 1967, Tijerina's group raided a courthouse in Tierra Amarilla, New Mexico—another land grant—and tried to arrest the local district attorney for violating members' civil rights.

CESAR CHAVEZ AND DOLORES HUERTA

Perhaps the most well-known event of the movement was led by Cesar Chavez and Dolores Huerta in the grape fields of California. In 1962, labor leaders Chavez and Huerta founded the National Farm Workers Association. This later became known as the United Farm Workers of America.

In 1965, Chavez and Huerta organized a strike by California grape pickers and asked the nation to **boycott** California grapes. They started gaining support from the public, which eventually led to other boycotts against lettuce growers and wine makers. This led to the passage of the Agricultural Labor Relations Act in 1975. This act gave the farmworkers the right to collective bargaining, or to working as a group to set up their conditions of employment.

Cesar Chavez

After his death in 1993, Chavez was awarded the Presidential Medal of Freedom. Dolores Huerta was awarded this honor in 2012.

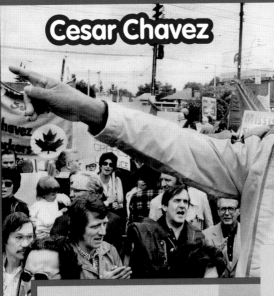

Dolores Huerta

EAST LOS ANGELES STUDENT WALKOUT

Mexican American students faced racism in their schools in East Los Angeles in the 1960s. They weren't allowed to speak Spanish in class and lessons didn't include Latino history. Some teachers even discouraged Mexican Americans from going to college, directing them instead toward unskilled work.

In 1968, a group of Mexican American students, along with teacher Sal Castro, gave the Board of Education a list of demands that included more Spanish-speaking teachers, **bilingual** classes and textbooks, and better buildings. These demands were not met, so Castro, the students, and movement activists organized a huge walkout of thousands of students in five high schools in East Los Angeles. The students were met with a violent response from the police.

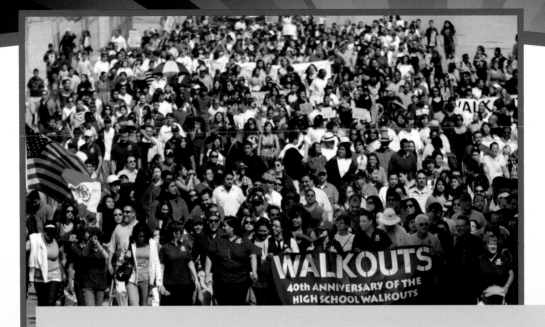

After the walkouts, more Latino teachers were hired, and college prep courses were made available to Mexican Americans. The Bilingual Education Act in 1968 guaranteed special programs for districts with high numbers of Spanish-speaking students.

The Protests Continue

After a week of protests, the Board of Education met with the striking students and agreed that changes were needed. However, 13 protesters, including Sal Castro, were arrested and charged with **conspiracy**, and Castro lost his job. Students began protesting at the district headquarters and the Hall of Justice in downtown Los Angeles. They gained the support of Senator Robert Kennedy and Cesar Chavez. Students then organized an eight-day **sit-in** at the Board of Education office.

OUTCOMES OF THE MOVEMENT

The Chicano movement was at its strongest during the 1960s and early 1970s. Although most Latino civil rights groups declined because of loss of funding, the impact of the movement continued into the 1980s. In 1986, the Immigration Reform and Control Act was passed. This gave the chance for legal citizenship to certain undocumented workers, including farm workers. In 1989, Dr. Lauro Cavazos was appointed Secretary of Education and became the first Latino to serve on a U.S. president's cabinet.

In 2006, Mexican American activists set up demonstrations across the country in response to proposals in Congress that would make undocumented immigrants criminals. These were the largest demonstrations in the United States since the late 1960s and early 1970s.

In 1994, Proposition 187, which denied many forms of public assistance for undocumented immigrants, was passed in California. This was met with massive protests and Proposition 187 was overturned in 1997.

Marches in 2006

Between March and May 2006, almost a million protesters marched against the proposals that would affect undocumented immigrants. Marches happened in major cities including Los Angeles, Dallas, and Chicago. Many of the organizers and participants of these rallies were high school and college students who used social media and text messaging to spread the word. Spanish-speaking newspapers and television stations also helped get the message out about the protests.

FUTURE OF THE MOVEMENT

Although Mexican American rights have come a long way since the days of Manifest Destiny, there's a long way to go. Latinos are the largest minority group in the United States, yet many still face inequality when it comes to jobs, housing, and educational opportunities. Another top issue for Mexican American activists is the treatment of undocumented immigrants, who are still the victims of racism and stereotyping.

The Mexican American civil rights movement is a continuing story of people fighting to earn their right to live in this country as equals. It's the story of migrant workers in the fields and Latino students and educators who decided to stand up for justice. Each new generation of Mexican Americans brings new life to the battle for social equality.

You can participate in the movement for equal rights by accepting people of all races and backgrounds. Ask your classmates and friends about their traditions and family history.

TIMELINE OF THE MEXICAN AMERICAN RIGHTS MOVEMENT

1848
The Treaty of Guadalupe Hidalgo is signed, guaranteeing constitutional rights for Mexicans living within the new U.S. borders after the U.S.-Mexican War.

1943
In Los Angeles, military men begin a week-long series of attacks on young Mexican Americans. These attacks become known as the "Zoot Suit Riots" because of the clothes many of the youth wear.

1947
After hearing the *Mendez v. Westminster* case, a judge rules that segregated schools violate the 14th Amendment and are unconstitutional.

1954
In the case of *Hernandez v. Texas*, the U.S. Supreme Court rules that a Mexican American man must be tried in front of a jury that wasn't selected based on race. Mexican Americans didn't serve on juries until this time.

1962
Cesar Chavez and Dolores Huerta create the National Farm Workers Association, which later becomes the United Farm Workers union.

1968
The East L.A. school walkouts begin. They are organized by Mexican American students and teacher Sal Castro.

1975
The Voting Rights Act is expanded to include Latinos.

1994
Proposition 187 is passed in California. It denies undocumented immigrants access to government programs such as food stamps and healthcare.

2006
Tens of thousands of Latinos protest proposals made in Congress that would make undocumented immigrants criminals.

GLOSSARY

access: The ability to use or enter something.

activist: Someone who acts strongly in support of or against an issue.

bilingual: Having to do with two languages.

boycott: To join with others in refusing to buy from or deal with a person, nation, or business.

conspiracy: The act of secretly planning to do something that is illegal or harmful.

discrimination: Treating people unequally because of their race, beliefs, background, or other factors.

land grant: An area of land that is given by the government to a person, organization, or a particular group of people.

minority: A group of people who are different from a larger population in some way.

racism: The belief that people of different races have different qualities and abilities and that some are superior or inferior.

segregation: The forced separation of people based on race, class, or ethnicity.

sit-in: A protest in which people sit or stay in a place and refuse to leave.

stereotype: An unfair belief that all people with a certain characteristic are the same.

undocumented: Not having the official documents that are needed to enter, live in, or work in a country legally.

violation: The act of ignoring or interfering with a person's rights; the act of doing something not allowed by a law or rule.

INDEX

WEBSITES

Due to the changing nature of Internet links, PowerKids Press has developed an online list of websites related to the subject of this book. This site is updated regularly. Please use this link to access the list: www.powerkidslinks.com/civic/mex